Let Freedom Ring

The Plymouth Colony

by Pamela Dell

Consultant:
Marsha Hamilton
Assistant Professor of History
University of South Alabama
Mobile, Alabama

Capstone press
Mankato, Minnesota

Capstone Press
151 Good Counsel Drive, P.O. Box 669, Mankato, Minnesota 56002
www.capstonepress.com

Library of Congress Cataloging-in-Publication Data
Dell, Pamela.
    The Plymouth Colony / by Pamela Dell.
    p. cm.—(Let freedom ring)
    Summary: Follows the struggles and triumphs of the colonists who came to the New
World and founded Plymouth Colony in what would become Massachusetts.
    Includes bibliographical references (p. 45) and index.
    ISBN 0-7368-2463-4 (hardcover)
    1. Massachusetts—History—New Plymouth, 1620–1691—Juvenile literature. 2.
Pilgrims (New Plymouth Colony)—Juvenile literature. [1. Massachusetts—History—New
Plymouth, 1620–1691. 2. Pilgrims (New Plymouth Colony)] I. Title. II. Series.
F68.D45 2004
974.4'02—dc22   2003012136

Editorial Credits
Katy Kudela, editor; Kia Adams, series designer; Molly Nei, book designer and illustrator;
    Scott Thoms, photo researcher; Eric Kudalis, product planning editor

Photo Credits
Cover image: Painting of Pilgrims landing at Plymouth by Currier and Ives,
Getty Images/Hulton Archive

Corbis, 15, 21, 27, 42; Bettmann, 5, 12, 32, 38, 43; Lake County Museum, 29
Getty Images/Hulton Archive, 7, 31, 37
The Granger Collection, New York, 19, 23, 24, 25, 30
Houserstock/Dave G. Houser, 41
North Wind Picture Archives, 10, 35
Courtesy of Pilgrim Hall Museum, Plymouth, Massachusetts, 9
Photri-Microstock, 13

1   2   3   4   5   6   09   08   07   06   05   04

Table of Contents

Chapter One

Land, Ahoy!

In November 1620, the passengers on board the *Mayflower* sighted land. The land was Cape Cod, in what is now the state of Massachusetts. Cape Cod was a welcome sight for the men, women, and children on board.

The *Mayflower*'s passengers set sail from England in September 1620. During the voyage, they braved the harsh waters of the Atlantic Ocean. They faced violent storms and damage to their ship. Many passengers suffered from seasickness.

The passengers' faith and courage kept them from turning back. They wanted to start a new life. Some were looking for religious freedom. Others were hoping to find riches.

The *Mayflower*'s journey across the Atlantic Ocean took at least 60 days.

The Pilgrims

Two groups of people sailed together on the *Mayflower*. These groups were known as the "Separatists" and the "Strangers."

Early in the 1600s, King James I of England announced his religious views. Anyone who did not worship in the Church of England could be punished. The Separatists wanted to separate themselves from the Church of England.

Fearing for their lives, many Separatists fled to Holland in 1608. The Separatists did not speak the Dutch language. Work was not easy to find. The Separatists set their hopes on present-day Virginia. A small group sailed from Holland back to England.

In London, the Separatists joined people eager to travel. The Separatists called this group "Strangers." Many of the Strangers were hoping to find riches. Most of the Strangers did not share the Separatists' religious views. They did share the hope of a better life elsewhere. Together these travelers became known as the **Pilgrims**.

In August 1620, the Pilgrims left England on board the *Mayflower* and the *Speedwell*. But the

Speedwell ran into trouble. The ships returned to England. After a second failed attempt to sail, the *Speedwell* was declared unsafe for the journey. Some of the *Speedwell*'s passengers decided not to travel. Others joined the passengers on the *Mayflower*. The *Mayflower* set sail a third time. This time the *Mayflower* sailed alone.

The *Mayflower* set sail from England in September 1620. To reach present-day America, the ship traveled 2,900 miles (4,667 kilometers).

Chapter Two

Finding Common Ground

In its voyage to North America, the *Mayflower* went badly off course. The Pilgrims had planned to settle in the area of present-day Virginia. As they sailed closer to shore in November 1620, the *Mayflower*'s passengers found they were well north of Virginia. The *Mayflower*'s captain tried to sail the ship south toward present-day Virginia.

Cape Cod Instead of Virginia

Fierce tides and wild currents forced the *Mayflower* to turn back. The ship anchored in Cape Cod Bay. With winter coming, the passengers gave up hope of reaching Virginia.

The Pilgrims had hoped to reach new land in time to plant crops. They wanted a fall harvest to feed them through the winter season.

The Pilgrims reached land in November 1620. Henry A. Bacon's 1877 painting shows the Pilgrims stepping onto Plymouth Rock.

The Pilgrims did not succeed in their plan. By the time they reached Cape Cod, winter was already on its way. The view before them was cold and empty. From the ship, the land appeared full of hidden dangers.

The Pilgrims were tired and weakened from the long journey. After landing in Cape Cod Bay, they were faced with the decision of where to settle the colony.

The Merchant Adventurers

The Pilgrims' trip was funded by a group of English businesspeople, known as merchant adventurers. These men agreed to stock the ships with supplies. They would also provide the Pilgrims with funds to build a colony. In return, the Pilgrims agreed to work for seven years to pay off these debts.

The Pilgrims hoped to work off a great deal of their debt. They planned to ship goods, such as lumber and furs, back to England. But the Pilgrims were not knowledgeable businesspeople. It took them until 1648 to pay their debt to the merchant adventurers.

Conflict Breaks Out

The Pilgrims' decision to settle a colony caused problems. Arguments broke out between the Separatists and Strangers. A colony in New England was outside their legal land **grant**.

Many of the Strangers felt free of the conditions they agreed to in England. They wanted to go their own way. They did not want to be part of a colony. The Separatists knew the colony needed people to succeed. The Pilgrims needed to find a solution before anyone was allowed to leave ship.

Men aboard the *Mayflower* signed the Mayflower Compact. Edward Moran's painting illustrates Miles Standish (middle, standing) helping William Bradford (right, with pen) sign the agreement.

A Necessary Agreement

The Pilgrims knew they needed rules for the colony. To settle their dispute, the Pilgrims created a document called the Mayflower Compact. This document declared that written laws would equally protect everyone. Anyone who signed the compact would agree to obey these laws. The Mayflower Compact also stated that a governor would be elected for the colony. All the men in the colony would have an equal vote in the election.

In November 1620, the 41 men on board the ship gathered together to hear the Mayflower Compact read aloud. Then each man signed the document to show his agreement. After signing the compact, the men elected John Carver as their governor. Carver was a respected Separatist.

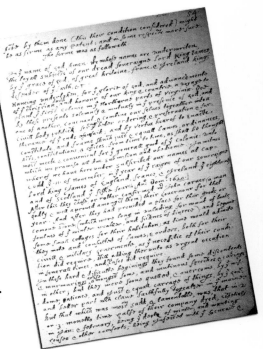

Mayflower Compact

Chapter Three

A Hard Winter

The Pilgrims were eager to set foot on land again. Many were ill or weakened from the difficult journey. The food and other supplies on board were running low. Shelters had to be built before the snow came. The **colonists** still had to decide the best place to build a permanent colony.

A Place to Settle

The Pilgrims anchored the *Mayflower* in the shelter of Cape Cod Bay. Some of the men made several expeditions to land. On these trips they found fresh springs of water. The Pilgrims also found baskets of multicolored corn. Indians had buried it in the ground.

The Pilgrims' expeditions caused trouble for the American Indians. The corn the colonists took was food the Indians had stored for the winter months.

The Pilgrims hoped to find food and shelter on Cape Cod.

The Pilgrims rarely saw American Indians. During their explorations, the men did find shelters made by the American Indians. But for the most part, the American Indians stayed away.

Moving On

The Pilgrims soon decided that Cape Cod was not a good site for their colony. Crops did not grow well in the sandy soil.

After a number of longer trips, the men discovered a better location. Plymouth was an area located west of Cape Cod. The area was on high ground and had a small bay of its own. The soil was rich. The area had many freshwater streams and dense woods. Also, it appeared that American Indians had recently lived there. Much of the land was already cleared. Planting crops and building homes would be easier.

A Difficult Time

The *Mayflower* dropped anchor in Plymouth Bay in December 1620. The Pilgrims traveled to shore in small boats. In the following days, men built shelters.

Plymouth Colony, 1620s

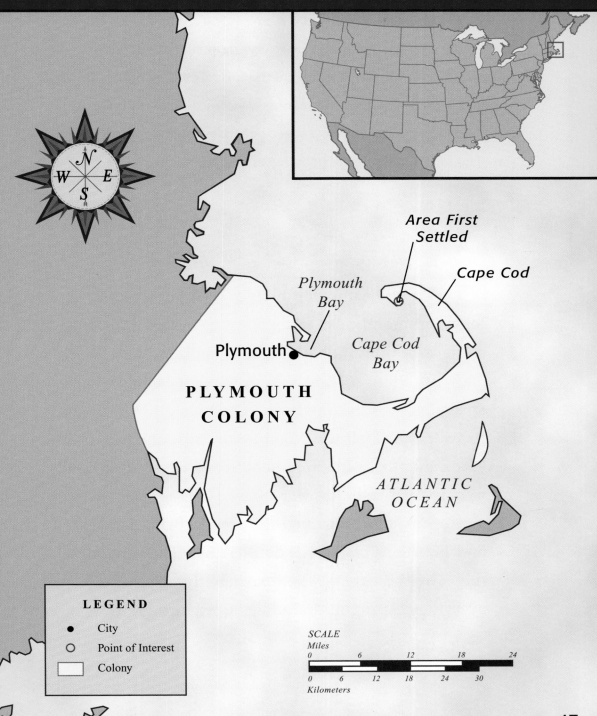

Area First Settled

Cape Cod

Plymouth Bay

Plymouth

Cape Cod Bay

PLYMOUTH COLONY

ATLANTIC OCEAN

LEGEND

● City

○ Point of Interest

▢ Colony

SCALE
Miles

| 0 | 6 | 12 | 18 | 24 |

| 0 | 6 | 12 | 18 | 24 | 30 |

Kilometers

The Great Sickness

During the first winter, many settlers became ill with **pneumonia**, a disease that infects the lungs. Others suffered from **scurvy**, a deadly disease that causes swollen limbs, bleeding gums, and weakness. By the end of February, only about 50 of the original 102 *Mayflower* passengers remained alive.

The Pilgrims first built a 20-foot (6-meter) long common house. This house provided shelter while they built individual family homes.

Building shelters was only one of many struggles the Pilgrims faced. Diseases quickly began to sweep through the colony. At times, only six or seven Pilgrims remained healthy. These settlers had to care for those that were ill.

Sickness continued to spread during January and February of 1621. The Pilgrims called this time the "Great Sickness." People were dying almost every day. At night, the bodies were buried in unmarked graves. The **survivors** wanted to hide the number of deaths. They believed the American Indians would attack if they knew how small the settlers' group had become.

The Pilgrims' first winter was harsh. The Pilgrims did not have proper shelters or supplies. Many people became ill and died.

Chapter Four

Peace with American Indians

As the spring of 1621 approached, work still needed to be done. Homes needed to be built. Many people were still sick and needed care day and night. The ship's supplies were nearly gone. Finding food was a constant concern for the Pilgrims.

Fish and game were plentiful, but the Pilgrims were farmers and traders. They were not skilled in hunting or fishing. Even their English fishhooks were too big to catch fish in the bay. The Pilgrims needed to learn new skills.

A Surprise Visit

In March 1621, the Pilgrims were surprised to see a tall, longhaired Indian man walk into the colony. He carried a bow and arrows.

During the spring of 1621, the Pilgrims were busy building homes. Unlike this artist's painting, the Pilgrims did not build log cabins.

The colonists were even more surprised when the man spoke to them in English. The man introduced himself as Samoset, a member of the Abenaki tribe in Maine. Samoset had learned to speak English from fishermen along the coast of Maine.

The colonists spoke with Samoset all afternoon. Samoset told the Pilgrims that the nearby Wampanoag Indians could be trusted. But he warned of other unfriendly tribes in the area.

Samoset told the settlers that the colony was built on land used by the Patuxet tribe. The land had been abandoned when a deadly illness killed nearly all of the tribe's members. The land remained empty because other tribes feared the area.

Samoset left the next morning, but he came to the colony several more times. He brought other men with him. One of these men was Squanto, a Patuxet Indian.

Squanto and the Pilgrims

Squanto spoke English well. He helped the Pilgrims talk with other American Indians. He also taught the Pilgrims many important skills.

Squanto shared his knowledge of farming and hunting. He also taught the Pilgrims fishing skills.

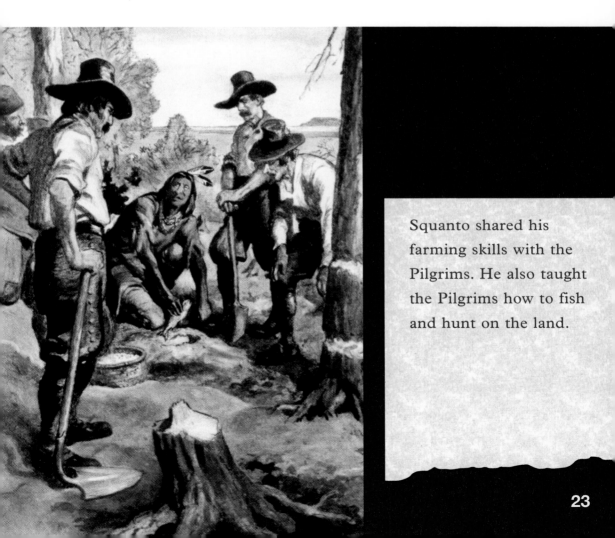

Squanto shared his farming skills with the Pilgrims. He also taught the Pilgrims how to fish and hunt on the land.

The Pilgrims learned the best ways to catch fish. They also learned to tell when the fish swam down the streams. Squanto soon became an important part of Plymouth Colony.

Chief Massasoit wished to create peace with the Pilgrims. He traveled with Samoset and Squanto to Plymouth Colony.

Squanto

Squanto was a member of the Patuxet tribe. He was also known by his Indian name of Tisquantum.

In 1614, Thomas Hunt, an English sea captain, kidnapped Squanto. Squanto was taken to Spain where Hunt planned to sell him as a slave. Local priests rescued Squanto. In 1618, Squanto traveled back to England. During his time in England, Squanto learned to speak English.

Squanto returned to his homeland in 1619. A grim sight awaited him there. There was no trace of the Patuxet village he called home. An unknown disease from Europe killed Squanto's people. Fishermen and explorers unknowingly brought this disease with them. The few remaining members of his tribe went to live with the Wampanoag. Upon his return home, Squanto also lived with the Wampanoag tribe.

Squanto played an important role in Plymouth Colony. He served as an interpreter between the Pilgrims and Wampanoag.

A Peace Treaty is Made

During another visit, Samoset came with Massasoit, a Wampanoag chief. Massasoit wanted to establish peace with the Pilgrims. He also asked for the Pilgrims' help in fighting against unfriendly tribes.

Governor John Carver agreed to meet with Massasoit. Squanto also attended the meeting. He served as an interpreter for the men.

During the meeting, the Wampanoag and Pilgrims created a peace **treaty**. The peace treaty listed several terms. The two groups agreed not to harm one another. They planned to join together to fight against attacks from others. The two groups also agreed to meet unarmed.

The peace treaty with Massasoit began in 1621. The peace treaty remained in place until after Massasoit's death in 1661.

Chief Massasoit met with Governor John Carver in 1621.
The Wampanoag and Pilgrims agreed to a peace treaty.

Chapter Five

Alone in a New Land

The *Mayflower* crew planned to leave Plymouth after landing the passengers. The group of sailors hoped to return to England. But the Pilgrims feared attacks from American Indians. They wanted a safe place to retreat. The *Mayflower* was the only safe place they had. For that reason, the captain agreed to Governor Carver's demand that the ship not leave immediately. The captain also knew he did not have enough men to sail the *Mayflower* back to England. Diseases continued to spread through the colony. Many sailors were ill.

By April, the remaining sailors had recovered. The colonists had the security of their peace treaty with the Wampanoag. They were busy building their **settlement**. It was time for the *Mayflower* to lift anchor and head back to England.

The Pilgrims watched as the *Mayflower* set sail for England in April 1621. The artist of this painting is George Henry Boughton.

In April 1621, the *Mayflower* sailed out of
Cape Cod Bay. The ship was the Pilgrims' last tie
to England. They were completely alone in the
wilderness of North America.

Alone in a new land, the Pilgrims' faith kept them strong. Going to
church was an important part of the Pilgrims' life.

Plymouth's Leaders

Many people helped keep Plymouth Colony going. Two of the best-remembered names are Miles Standish and William Bradford. These men were both important figures in Plymouth's history.

Miles Standish was a professional military man. At Plymouth Colony, he was elected captain of the men. He was given the authority to take command in times of danger. Later, Standish became a political leader in the colony. He served as the colony's treasurer and became an advisor to the governor.

Miles Standish

William Bradford, a Separatist, came from northern England. His hope was to see Plymouth grow through its members' faith in God. Bradford always put the interests of the colony first. He was a loved and respected leader. He served as Plymouth's governor for 36 years.

The death of Governor John Carver brought sadness to Plymouth
Colony. The Pilgrims' faith again helped them through a difficult time.
Jean Leon Gerome Ferris' painting shows the Pilgrims in prayer.

A Change in Leadership

More changes came to the colony in April 1621. While working under the hot sun, Governor Carver became ill. He died a few days later. Carver had been a trusted leader, and his death was a tragic loss for the colony. In his place, the Pilgrims elected William Bradford as their governor. He remained Plymouth's governor until his death in 1657.

Harvest

The Pilgrims worked hard during the summer. Most of the seeds they brought from England did not grow. But their corn and other native crops grew. The Pilgrims became more skilled at fishing and hunting. With the warmer weather, the Pilgrims also had berries and other wild fruits to eat. In the fall, the colonists harvested 20 acres (8 hectares) of Indian corn and 6 acres (2.4 hectares) of peas and barley.

The Pilgrims felt their faith in God had seen them through many troubles. In October, Governor Bradford called for a great celebration for all of their blessings. The feast lasted three days.

The harvest feast included many foods. The men went hunting and brought back geese and ducks. They caught lobster, eel, and shellfish. The women baked corn bread, meat pies, and puddings.

The colonists were confident there would be plenty of food. But they did not expect a large number of guests. Governor Bradford invited Massasoit to the feast. Massasoit arrived with 90 men from his tribe. When Massasoit saw that the Pilgrims were not prepared, he sent some of his men out to hunt. These men returned with five deer. This deer meat provided enough food for everyone.

The colonists continued this harvest tradition every year. Today, the United States' national Thanksgiving holiday reminds people of the Pilgrims' experience. But Thanksgiving did not become an official holiday until nearly 250 years after that first celebration. In 1863, President Abraham Lincoln pronounced the fourth Thursday in November to be a national day of giving thanks in the United States.

Artists' Views of Thanksgiving

Many artists have drawn images of the Pilgrims' first Thanksgiving. These artists have included their own ideas. But many of these ideas are based on myth.

Historians have found only two written accounts of the Pilgrims' first Thanksgiving. Colonist Edward Winslow wrote about the feast in a letter dated December 12, 1621. Later, William Bradford also provided information in his book *History of Plymouth Plantation*.

Chapter Six

Struggling to Survive

As time went on, the colonists faced more difficulties. The Pilgrims worried about the number of new colonists coming to New England's shores.

The English newcomers often arrived without supplies. Many expected the Plymouth colonists to provide food and other supplies. The Pilgrims helped the new colonists, but the Pilgrims quickly ran out of supplies.

Some of the new settlers were **Puritans**. Like the Pilgrims, the Puritans had a strong interest in owning land. They also wanted to earn money through the trade industry. The Puritans began to take away business from the Pilgrims. The Pilgrims struggled to earn money.

As Plymouth Colony grew, so did the Pilgrims' worries. They faced a lack of food and supplies.

All around Plymouth, the French and the Dutch were setting up trading posts and trapping for furs. These trading posts also took away from the Pilgrims' profits. The new colonies were growing quickly. But the Pilgrims were poor and hungry.

The End of Plymouth Colony

During its later years, Plymouth faced many troubles. New colonies had formed in the area. Land and trade arguments broke out among the colonies. The Plymouth colonists feared attacks

Dutch settlers were among the new settlers to arrive in Plymouth Colony. The Dutch set up trading posts and trapped woodland animals for fur.

Newcomers

The first of many ships to arrive at Plymouth after the *Mayflower*'s departure was the *Fortune*. The *Fortune* landed in November 1621, carrying 35 English passengers. Many of these passengers were young men. For the most part, these men did not share the Separatists' dedication to religion. To make matters more difficult, the *Fortune* carried few supplies.

The original colonists had just begun to feel a bit of security and comfort. The arrival of the *Fortune* changed the Pilgrims' lives. The governor of Plymouth Colony ordered the Pilgrims to share their food and supplies.

The settlers aboard the *Fortune* were the first of many groups the Pilgrims helped. The Pilgrims always found ways to provide for the newcomers.

from nearby Dutch colonists. They were also fearful of attacks from American Indians.

In 1643, Plymouth and other nearby colonies formed the United Colonies of New England. Other colonies in this union included Massachusetts Bay,

Connecticut, and New Haven. The colonies helped each other settle arguments and fight other groups.

In 1686, England tried to gain control over the colonies. King James II of England united all of New England under one government. He named this area the Dominion of New England. In 1688, he added the colonies of New York and New Jersey. The Dominion of New England lasted from 1686 to 1689. In 1691, Plymouth became part of the Massachusetts Bay Colony.

Learning from Plymouth

More than 350 years ago, colonists settled Plymouth Colony. Today, people can learn about this colony's importance at Plimoth Plantation. This living history museum is located on the site of the original Plymouth Colony. Workers at the museum show visitors colonial life in 1627.

Plymouth Colony was successful in many ways. The colony served as a model for other colonies. The Pilgrims' belief in hard work, trust in their faith, and service to others are still part of American culture.

Many people visit Plimoth Plantation in Plymouth, Massachusetts. The living history museum offers visitors a view of colonial life in 1627.

TIME LINE

September—The
Mayflower leaves
for North America.

November—The
Mayflower drops anchor
in Cape Cod Bay.

March—Samoset speaks
with the Pilgrims;
Pilgrims create a peace
treaty with Wampanoag.

A group of Separatists
emigrate to Holland.

1608	1620	1621

October—The Pilgrims
celebrate their first
harvest Thanksgiving
in Plymouth.

December—Pilgrims anchor ship
in Plymouth Bay.

Late December—Pilgrims begin
building their colony.

William Bradford dies from an illness; he served as Plymouth's governor for 36 years.

Plymouth Colony becomes part of the Massachusetts Bay Colony.

| 1648 | 1657 | 1661 | 1691 |

Chief Massasoit dies; the Pilgrims begin to have increased troubles with the Wampanoag and other American Indians.

The colonists pay their debt in full to the merchant adventurers in London.

Glossary

colonist (KOL-uh-nist)—person who makes a home in a new area

grant (GRANT)—a gift such as land or money given for a particular purpose

Pilgrim (PIL-gruhm)—one of the English Separatists or Strangers who settled in North America in 1620

pneumonia (noo-MOH-nyuh)—a disease that causes the lungs to become infected and fill with liquid

Puritan (PYOOR-uh-tuhn)—one of a group of Protestants in the 1500s and 1600s who sought simple church services and a strict moral code; many Puritans fled England and settled in North America.

scurvy (SKUR-vee)—a deadly disease caused by lack of vitamin C; scurvy produces swollen limbs, bleeding gums, and weakness.

settlement (SET-uhl-muhnt)—a colony or group of people who have left one place to make a home in another place

survivor (sur-VYE-vur)—someone who lives through a disaster or horrible event

treaty (TREE-tee)—an official agreement between two or more groups or countries

Read More

Collier, Christopher, and James Lincoln Collier. *Pilgrims and Puritans: 1620–1676.* The Drama of American History. New York: Benchmark Books, 1998.

Grace, Catherine O'Neill, and Margaret M. Bruchac, with Plimoth Plantation. *1621: A New Look at Thanksgiving.* Washington, D.C.: National Geographic Society, 2001.

Santella, Andrew. *The Plymouth Colony.* We the People. Minneapolis: Compass Point Books, 2001.

Schmidt, Gary D. *William Bradford: Plymouth's Faithful Pilgrim.* Grand Rapids, Mich.: Eerdmans Books for Young Readers, 1999.

Witteman, Barbara. *Miles Standish: Colonial Leader.* Let Freedom Ring. Mankato, Minn.: Bridgestone Books, 2004.

Useful Addresses

Miles Standish Monument
Crescent Street
Duxbury, MA 02332
This monument in Duxbury
was built in honor of Miles
Standish, a military leader in
Plymouth Colony.

**National Monument to
the Forefathers**
Allerton Street
Plymouth, MA 02360
Built to honor Plymouth's
founders, this monument in
Plymouth is one of the largest
statues in the United States. It
stands 81 feet (25 meters) tall.
The names of the *Mayflower*'s
passengers are etched into
the stone.

Pilgrim Hall Museum
75 Court Street
Plymouth, MA 02360
This museum houses the world's
largest and most complete
collection of Pilgrim artifacts.

Plimoth Plantation
137 Warren Avenue
P.O. Box 1620
Plymouth, MA 02362
This outdoor living history
museum is built on the actual site
of the original Plymouth Colony.
Visitors to this museum can learn
about life in Plymouth Colony
in 1627.

Internet Sites

Facthound offers a safe, fun way to find Internet sites related to this book. All of the sites on Facthound have been researched by our staff.

Here's how:
1. Visit *www.facthound.com*
2. Type in this special code **0736824634** for age-appropriate sites.
   Or enter a search word related to this book for a more general search.
3. Click on the Fetch It button.

Facthound will fetch the best sites for you!

Index